I0469081

The Key Facts™

on

Brazil

Essential Information on Brazil

By Patrick W. Nee

The Internationalist®

www.internationalist.com

<u>**The Internationalist**</u>®

International Business, Investment, and Travel

Published by:

The Internationalist Publishing Company

96 Walter Street/ Suite 200

Boston, MA 02131, USA

Tel: 617-354-7722

www.internationalist.com

PN@internationalist.com

Copyright © 2013 by PWN

The Internationalist is a Registered Trademark. "Key Facts" and "The Internationalist Business Guides" are Trademarks of The Internationalist Publishing Company.

All Rights are reserved under International, Pan-American, and Pan-Asian Conventions. No part of this book may be reproduced in any form without the written permission of the publisher. All rights vigorously enforced

Table Of Contents

Chapter 1: Background

Following more than three centuries under Portuguese rule, Brazil gained its independence in 1822, maintaining a monarchical system of government until the abolition of slavery in 1888 and the subsequent proclamation of a republic by the military in 1889. Brazilian coffee exporters politically dominated the country until populist leader Getulio VARGAS rose to power in 1930. By far the largest and most populous country in South America, Brazil underwent more than a half century of populist and military government until 1985, when the military regime peacefully ceded power to civilian rulers. Brazil continues to pursue industrial and agricultural growth and development of its interior. Exploiting vast natural resources and a large labor pool, it is today South America's leading economic power and a regional leader, one of the first in the area to begin an economic recovery. Highly unequal income distribution and crime remain pressing problems.

Chapter 2: Geography

Location:

Eastern South America, bordering the Atlantic Ocean

Geographic coordinates:

10 00 S, 55 00 W

Map references:

South America

Area:

total: 8,514,877 sq km

country comparison to the world: 5

land: 8,459,417 sq km

water: 55,460 sq km

note: includes Arquipelago de Fernando de Noronha, Atol das Rocas, Ilha da Trindade, Ilhas Martin Vaz, and Penedos de Sao Pedro e Sao Paulo

Area - comparative:

slightly smaller than the US

Land boundaries:

total: 16,885 km

border countries: Argentina 1,261 km, Bolivia 3,423 km, Colombia 1,644 km, French Guiana 730 km, Guyana 1,606 km, Paraguay 1,365 km, Peru 2,995 km, Suriname 593 km, Uruguay 1,068 km, Venezuela 2,200 km

Coastline:

7,491 km

Maritime claims:

    territorial sea: 12 nm

    contiguous zone: 24 nm

    exclusive economic zone: 200 nm

    continental shelf: 200 nm or to edge of the continental margin

Climate:

    mostly tropical, but temperate in south

Terrain:

    mostly flat to rolling lowlands in north; some plains, hills, mountains, and narrow coastal belt

Elevation extremes:

    lowest point: Atlantic Ocean 0 m

    highest point: Pico da Neblina 2,994 m

Natural resources:

    bauxite, gold, iron ore, manganese, nickel, phosphates, platinum, tin, rare earth elements, uranium, petroleum, hydropower, timber

Land use:

    arable land: 6.93%

    permanent crops: 0.89%

    other: 92.18% (2005)

Irrigated land:

    45,000 sq km (2003)

Total renewable water resources:

    8,233 cu km (2000)

Freshwater withdrawal (domestic/industrial/agricultural):

total: 59.3 cu km/yr (20%/18%/62%)

per capita: 318 cu m/yr (2000)

Natural hazards:

recurring droughts in northeast; floods and occasional frost in south

Environment - current issues:

deforestation in Amazon Basin destroys the habitat and endangers a multitude of plant and animal species indigenous to the area; there is a lucrative illegal wildlife trade; air and water pollution in Rio de Janeiro, Sao Paulo, and several other large cities; land degradation and water pollution caused by improper mining activities; wetland degradation; severe oil spills

Environment - international agreements:

party to: Antarctic-Environmental Protocol, Antarctic-Marine Living Resources, Antarctic Seals, Antarctic Treaty, Biodiversity, Climate Change, Climate Change-Kyoto Protocol, Desertification, Endangered Species, Environmental Modification, Hazardous Wastes, Law of the Sea, Marine Dumping, Ozone Layer Protection, Ship Pollution, Tropical Timber 83, Tropical Timber 94, Wetlands, Whaling

signed, but not ratified: none of the selected agreements

Geography - note:

largest country in South America; shares common boundaries with every South American country except Chile and Ecuador

Chapter 3: People and Society

Nationality:

noun: Brazilian(s)

adjective: Brazilian

Ethnic groups:

white 53.7%, mulatto (mixed white and black) 38.5%,

black 6.2%, other (includes Japanese, Arab, Amerindian)

0.9%, unspecified 0.7% (2000 census)

Languages:

Portuguese (official and most widely spoken language)

note: less common languages include Spanish (border

areas and schools), German, Italian, Japanese, English, and

a large number of minor Amerindian languages

Religions:

Roman Catholic (nominal) 73.6%, Protestant 15.4%,

Spiritualist 1.3%, Bantu/voodoo 0.3%, other 1.8%,

unspecified 0.2%, none 7.4% (2000 census)

Demographic profile:

Brazil's rapid fertility decline since the 1960s is the main

factor behind the country's slowing population growth rate,

aging population, and fast-paced demographic transition.

Brasilia has not taken full advantage of its large working-

age population to develop its human capital and strengthen

its social and economic institutions. The current favorable

age structure will begin to shift around 2025, with the

labor force shrinking and the elderly starting to compose an increasing share of the total population. Well-funded public pensions have nearly wiped out poverty among the elderly, but limited social spending on children has restricted investment in education - a primary means of escaping poverty. Brazil's poverty and income inequality levels remain high despite improvements in the 2000s and continue to disproportionately affect the Northeast, North, and Center-West, women, and black, mixed race, and indigenous populations. Disparities in opportunities foster social exclusion and contribute to Brazil's high crime rate, particularly violent crime in cities and favelas.

Brazil has traditionally been a net recipient of immigrants, with its southeast being the prime destination. After the importation of African slaves was outlawed in the mid-19th century, Brazil sought Europeans (Italians, Portuguese, Spaniards, and Germans) and later Asians (Japanese) to work in agriculture, especially coffee cultivation. Recent immigrants come mainly from Argentina, Chile, and Andean countries (many are unskilled illegal migrants) or are returning Brazilian nationals. Since Brazil's economic downturn in the 1980s, emigration to the United States, Europe, and Japan has been rising but is negligible relative to Brazil's total population. The majority of these emigrants are well-educated and middle-class. Fewer Brazilian peasants are emigrating to neighboring countries to take up agricultural work.

Population:

199,321,413 (July 2012 est.)

country comparison to the world: 5

Age structure:

0-14 years: 24.7% (male 25,066,889/female 24,125,185)

15-24 years: 16.8% (male 17,002,355/female 16,535,115)

25-54 years: 43.4% (male 42,840,045/female 43,621,211)

55-64 years: 8% (male 7,522,621/female 8,441,593)

65 years and over: 7.1% (male 6,007,524/female 8,158,875) (2012 est.)

Median age:

total: 29.6 years

male: 28.8 years

female: 30.5 years (2012 est.)

Population growth rate:

0.86% (2012 est.)

country comparison to the world: 131

Birth rate:

15.2 births/1,000 population (2012 est.)

country comparison to the world: 132

Death rate:

6.5 deaths/1,000 population (July 2012 est.)

country comparison to the world: 149

Net migration rate:

-0.09 migrant(s)/1,000 population (2012 est.)

country comparison to the world: 120

Urbanization:

urban population: 87% of total population (2010)

rate of urbanization: 1.1% annual rate of change (2010-15 est.)

Major cities - population:

Sao Paulo 19.96 million; Rio de Janeiro 11.836 million; Belo Horizonte 5.736 million; Porto Alegre 4.034 million; BRASILIA (capital) 3.789 million (2009)

Sex ratio:

at birth: 1.05 male(s)/female

under 15 years: 1.04 male(s)/female

15-64 years: 0.98 male(s)/female

65 years and over: 0.74 male(s)/female

total population: 0.98 male(s)/female (2011 est.)

Maternal mortality rate:

56 deaths/100,000 live births (2010)

country comparison to the world: 104

Infant mortality rate:

total: 20.5 deaths/1,000 live births

country comparison to the world: 93

male: 23.9 deaths/1,000 live births

female: 16.9 deaths/1,000 live births (2012 est.)

Life expectancy at birth:

total population: 72.79 years

country comparison to the world: 124

male: 69.24 years

female: 76.53 years (2012 est.)

Total fertility rate:

1.82 children born/woman (2012 est.)

country comparison to the world: 153

Health expenditures:

9% of GDP (2009)

country comparison to the world: 44

Physicians density:

1.72 physicians/1,000 population (2007)

Hospital bed density:

2.4 beds/1,000 population (2009)

Sanitation facility access:

improved:

urban: 87% of population

rural: 37% of population

total: 80% of population

unimproved:

urban: 13% of population

rural: 63% of population

total: 20% of population

Obesity - adult prevalence rate:

11.1% (2003)

country comparison to the world: 52

Children under the age of 5 years underweight:

2.2% (2007)

country comparison to the world: 110

Education expenditures:

5% of GDP (2007)

country comparison to the world: 59

Literacy:

definition: age 15 and over can read and write

total population: 88.6%

male: 88.4%

female: 88.8% (2004 est.)

School life expectancy (primary to tertiary education):

total: 14 years

male: 14 years

female: 14 years (2008)

Unemployment, youth ages 15-24:

total: 17.8%

country comparison to the world: 66

male: 13.9%

female: 23.1% (2009)

Chapter 4: Government and Key Leaders

Country name:

> conventional long form: Federative Republic of Brazil
>
> conventional short form: Brazil
>
> local long form: Republica Federativa do Brasil
>
> local short form: Brasil

Government type:

> federal republic

Capital:

> name: Brasilia
>
> geographic coordinates: 15 47 S, 47 55 W
>
> time difference: UTC-3 (2 hours ahead of Washington, DC during Standard Time)
>
> daylight saving time: +1hr, begins third Sunday in October; ends third Sunday in February
>
> note: Brazil is divided into three time zones, including one for the Fernando de Noronha Islands

Administrative divisions:

> 26 states (estados, singular - estado) and 1 federal district* (distrito federal); Acre, Alagoas, Amapa, Amazonas, Bahia, Ceara, Distrito Federal*, Espirito Santo, Goias, Maranhao, Mato Grosso, Mato Grosso do Sul, Minas Gerais, Para, Paraiba, Parana, Pernambuco, Piaui, Rio de Janeiro, Rio Grande do Norte, Rio Grande do Sul,

Rondonia, Roraima, Santa Catarina, Sao Paulo, Sergipe, Tocantins

Independence:

7 September 1822 (from Portugal)

National holiday:

Independence Day, 7 September (1822)

Constitution:

5 October 1988

Legal system:

civil law; note - a new civil law code was enacted in 2002 replacing the 1916 code

International law organization participation:

has not submitted an ICJ jurisdiction declaration; accepts ICCt jurisdiction

Suffrage:

voluntary between 16 to under 18 years of age and over 70; compulsory 18 to 70 years of age; note - military conscripts do not vote by law

Executive branch:

chief of state: President Dilma ROUSSEFF (since 1 January 2011); Vice President Michel TEMER (since 1 January 2011); note - the president is both the chief of state and head of government

head of government: President Dilma ROUSSEFF (since 1 January 2011); Vice President Michel TEMER (since 1 January 2011) cabinet: Cabinet appointed by the president

elections: president and vice president elected on the same ticket by popular vote for a single four-year term; election last held on 3 October 2010 with runoff on 31 October 2010 (next to be held on 5 October 2014 and, if necessary, a runoff election on 2 November 2014)

election results: Dilma ROUSSEFF (PT) elected president in a runoff election; percent of vote - Dilma ROUSSEFF 56.01%, Jose SERRA (PSDB) 43.99%

Legislative branch:

bicameral National Congress or Congresso Nacional consists of the Federal Senate or Senado Federal (81 seats; 3 members from each state and federal district elected according to the principle of majority to serve eight-year terms; one-third and two-thirds of members elected every four years, alternately) and the Chamber of Deputies or Camara dos Deputados (513 seats; members are elected by proportional representation to serve four-year terms)

elections: Federal Senate - last held on 3 October 2010 for two-thirds of the Senate (next to be held in October 2014 for one-third of the Senate); Chamber of Deputies - last held on 3 October 2010 (next to be held in October 2014)

election results: Federal Senate - percent of vote by party - NA; seats by party - PMDB 20, PT 13, PSDB 10, DEM (formerly PFL) 7, PTdoB 6, PP 5, PDT 4, PR 4, PSB 4, PPS 1, PRB 1, other 3; Chamber of Deputies - percent of

vote by party - NA; seats by party - PT 87, PMDB 80,
PSDB 53, DEM (formerly PFL) 43, PP 41, PR 41, PSB
34, PDT 28, PTdoB 21, PSC 17, PCdoB 15, PV 15, PPS
12, other 18

Judicial branch:

Supreme Federal Tribunal or STF (11 ministers are
appointed for life by the president and confirmed by the
Senate); Superior Tribunal of Justice or STJ; Superior
Electoral Tribunal or TSE; Regional Federal Tribunals
(judges are appointed for life); note - though appointed
"for life," judges, like all federal employees, have a
mandatory retirement age of 70

Political parties and leaders:

Brazilian Democratic Movement Party or PMDB [Michel
TEMER]; Brazilian Labor Party or PTB [Roberto
JEFFERSON]; Brazilian Renewal Labor Party or PRTB
[Jose Levy FIDELIX da Cruz]; Brazilian Republican Party
or PRB [Vitor Paulo DOS SANTOS]; Brazilian Social
Democracy Party or PSDB [Sergio GUERRA]; Brazilian
Socialist Party or PSB [Eduardo Henrique Accioly
CAMPOS]; Christian Labor Party or PTC [Daniel
TOURINHO]; Communist Party of Brazil or PCdoB [Jose
Renato RABELO]; Democratic Labor Party or PDT
[Carlos Roberto LUPI]; the Democrats or DEM [Jose
AGRIPINO] (formerly Liberal Front Party or PFL);
Freedom and Socialism Party or PSOL [Ivan VALENTE];

Green Party or PV [Jose Luiz PENNA]; Humanist Party of
Solidarity or PHS [Philippe GUEDON]; Labor Party of
Brazil or PTdoB [Luis Henrique de Oliveira RESENDE];
National Mobilization Party or PMN [Celso BRANT];
Party of the Republic or PR [Sergio Victor TAMER];
Popular Socialist Party or PPS [Roberto Joao PEREIRA
FREIRE]; Progressive Party or PP [Francisco
DORNELLES]; Social Christian Party or PSC [Vitor Jorge
Abdala NOSSEIS]; Social Democracy Party or PSD
[Gilberto KASSAB]; Workers' Party or PT [Rui
FALCAO]

Political pressure groups and leaders:

Landless Workers' Movement or MST

other: industrial federations; labor unions and federations;
large farmers' associations; religious groups including
evangelical Christian churches and the Catholic Church

International organization participation:

AfDB (nonregional member), BIS, BRICS, CAN
(associate), CD, CELAC, CPLP, FAO, FATF, G-15, G-20,
G-24, G-77, IADB, IAEA, IBRD, ICAO, ICC (national
committees), ICRM, IDA, IFAD, IFC, IFRCS, IHO, ILO,
IMF, IMO, IMSO, Interpol, IOC, IOM, IPU, ISO, ITSO,
ITU, ITUC (NGOs), LAES, LAIA, LAS (observer),
Mercosur, MIGA, MINURSO, MINUSTAH, NAM
(observer), NSG, OAS, OECD (Enhanced Engagement,
OPANAL, OPCW, Paris Club (associate), PCA, SICA

(observer), UN, UNASUR, UNCTAD, UNESCO, UNFICYP, UNHCR, UNIDO, UNIFIL, Union Latina, UNISFA, UNITAR, UNMIL, UNMISS, UNMIT, UNOCI, UNWTO, UPU, WCO, WFTU (NGOs), WHO, WIPO, WMO, WTO

Diplomatic representation in the US:

chief of mission: Ambassador Mauro Luiz Iecker VIEIRA

chancery: 3006 Massachusetts Avenue NW, Washington, DC 20008

telephone: [1] (202) 238-2805

FAX: [1] (202) 238-2827

consulate(s) general: Atlanta, Boston, Chicago, Hartford, Houston, Los Angeles, Miami, New York, San Francisco

Diplomatic representation from the US:

chief of mission: Ambassador Thomas A. SHANNON

embassy: Avenida das Nacoes, Quadra 801, Lote 3, Distrito Federal Cep 70403-900, Brasilia

mailing address: Unit 7500, DPO, AA 34030

telephone: [55] (61) 3312-7000

FAX: [55] (61) 3225-9136

consulate(s) general: Rio de Janeiro, Sao Paulo

consulate(s): Recife

Key Leaders:

Pres.	Dilma ROUSSEFF
Vice Pres.	Michel TEMER
Chief of the Civilian Household of	Gleisi Helena HOFFMANN

the Presidency	
Sec. Gen. of the Presidency	Gilberto CARVALHO
Min. of Agrarian Development	Pepe VARGAS
Min. of Agriculture, Livestock, & Supply	Mendes RIBEIRO Filho
Min. of Cities	Aguinaldo RIBEIRO
Min. of Communications	Paulo BERNARDO
Min. of Culture	Marta SUPLICY
Min. of Defense	Celso Luiz Nunes AMORIM
Min. of Development, Industry, & Trade	Fernando Damata PIMENTEL
Min. of Education	Aloizio MERCADANTE Oliva
Min. of the Environment	Izabella TEIXEIRA
Min. of Finance	Guido MANTEGA
Min. of Fishing & Aquaculture	Marcello CRIVELLA
Min. of Foreign Relations	Antonio de Aguiar PATRIOTA
Min. of Health	Alexandre PADILHA
Min. of Justice	Jose Eduardo Martins CARDOZO
Min. of Labor & Employment	Carlos Daudt BRIZOLA
Min. of Mines & Energy	Edison LOBAO
Min. of National Integration	Fernando BEZERRA COELHO
Min. of Planning, Budget, & Management	Miriam Aparecida BELCHIOR

Min. of Science & Technology	Marco Antonio RAUPP
Min. of Social Development & Hunger Alleviation	Tereza CAMPELO
Min. of Social Security	Garibaldi ALVES FILHO
Min. of Sports	Aldo REBELO
Min. of Tourism	Gastao VIEIRA
Min. of Transportation	Paulo Sergio PASSOS
Head, Office of the Inspectorate Gen.	Jorge HAGE
Head, Office of Institutional Security	Jose ELITO Carvalho Siqueira
Head, Office of the Solicitor Gen.	Luis Inacio Lucena ADAMS
Head, Secretariat of Civil Aviation	Wagner BITTENCOURT
Head, Secretariat of Institutional Relations	Ideli SALVATTI
Head, Secretariat for Social Communication	Helena CHAGAS
Head, Secretariat of Strategic Affairs	Moreira FRANCO
Head, Special Secretariat for Human Rights	Maria do ROSARIO
Head, Special Secretariat for Promotion of Racial Equality	Luiza BAIRROS

Head, Special Secretariat for Women's Rights	Eleonora MENICUCCI de Oliveira
Head, Special Secretariat of Ports	Leonidas CRISTINO
Pres., Central Bank	Alexandre Antonio TOMBINI
Ambassador to the US	Mauro Luiz Iecker VIEIRA
Permanent Representative to the UN, New York	Maria Luiza Ribeiro VIOTTI

Flag description:

green with a large yellow diamond in the center bearing a blue celestial globe with 27 white five-pointed stars; the globe has a white equatorial band with the motto ORDEM E PROGRESSO (Order and Progress); the current flag was inspired by the banner of the former Empire of Brazil (1822-1889); on the imperial flag, the green represented the House of Braganza of Pedro I, the first Emperor of Brazil, while the yellow stood for the Habsburg Family of his wife; on the modern flag the green represents the forests of the country and the yellow rhombus its mineral wealth; the blue circle and stars, which replaced the coat of arms of the original flag, depict the sky over Rio de Janeiro on the morning of 15 November 1889 - the day the Republic of Brazil was declared; the number of stars has changed with the creation of new states and has risen from an original 21 to the current 27 (one for each state and the Federal District)

National symbol(s):

Southern Cross constellation

National anthem:

name: "Hino Nacional Brasileiro" (Brazilian National
Anthem)

lyrics/music: Joaquim Osorio Duque
ESTRADA/Francisco Manoel DA SILVA

note: music adopted 1890, lyrics adopted 1922; the
anthem's music, composed in 1822, was used unofficially
for many years before it was adopted

Chapter 5: Economy

Economy - overview:

Characterized by large and well-developed agricultural, mining, manufacturing, and service sectors, Brazil's economy outweighs that of all other South American countries, and Brazil is expanding its presence in world markets. Since 2003, Brazil has steadily improved its macroeconomic stability, building up foreign reserves, and reducing its debt profile by shifting its debt burden toward real denominated and domestically held instruments. In 2008, Brazil became a net external creditor and two ratings agencies awarded investment grade status to its debt. After strong growth in 2007 and 2008, the onset of the global financial crisis hit Brazil in 2008. Brazil experienced two quarters of recession, as global demand for Brazil's commodity-based exports dwindled and external credit dried up. However, Brazil was one of the first emerging markets to begin a recovery. In 2010, consumer and investor confidence revived and GDP growth reached 7.5%, the highest growth rate in the past 25 years. Rising inflation led the authorities to take measures to cool the economy; these actions and the deteriorating international economic situation slowed growth to 2.7% in 2011, and 1.5% in 2012. Despite slower growth, in 2011 Brazil overtook the United Kingdom as the world's seventh largest economy in terms of GDP. Unemployment is at historic lows and Brazil's traditionally high level of income inequality has declined for each of the last 14 years. Brazil's historically high interest rates have made it an attractive destination for foreign investors. Large capital inflows over the past several years have contributed to the appreciation of the currency, hurting the competitiveness of Brazilian manufacturing and leading the government to intervene in foreign exchanges markets and raise taxes on some foreign capital inflows. President Dilma ROUSSEFF has retained the previous administration's commitment to inflation targeting by the central bank, a floating exchange rate, and fiscal restraint. In an effort to boost growth, in 2012 the administration implemented a series of more expansionary monetary and fiscal policies that have failed to stimulate much growth.

GDP (purchasing power parity):

$2.362 trillion (2012 est.)

country comparison to the world: 8

$2.331 trillion (2011 est.)

$2.269 trillion (2010 est.)

note: data are in 2012 US dollars

GDP (official exchange rate):

$2.425 trillion (2012 est.)

GDP - real growth rate:

1.3% (2012 est.)

country comparison to the world: 155

2.7% (2011 est.)

7.5% (2010 est.)

GDP - per capita (PPP):

$12,000 (2012 est.)

country comparison to the world: 103

$12,000 (2011 est.)

$11,700 (2010 est.)

note: data are in 2012 US dollars

GDP - composition by sector:

agriculture: 5.4%

industry: 27.4%

services: 67.2% (2012 est.)

Labor force:

107.1 million (2012 est.)

country comparison to the world: 6

Labor force - by occupation:

agriculture: 20%

industry: 14%

services: 66% (2003 est.)

Unemployment rate:

6.2% (2012 est.)

country comparison to the world: 63

6% (2011 est.)

Population below poverty line:

21.4% (2009 est.)

Household income or consumption by percentage share:

lowest 10%: 0.8%

highest 10%: 42.9% (2009 est.)

Distribution of family income - Gini index:

51.9 (2012)

country comparison to the world: 16

60.7 (1998)

Investment (gross fixed):

18.9% of GDP (2012 est.)

country comparison to the world: 112

Budget:

revenues: $911.4 billion

expenditures: $846.6 billion (2012 est.)

Taxes and other revenues:

37.6% of GDP (2012 est.)

country comparison to the world: 59

Budget surplus (+) or deficit (-):

2.7% of GDP (2012 est.)

country comparison to the world: 19

Public debt:

54.9% of GDP (2012 est.)

country comparison to the world: 54

54.2% of GDP (2011 est.)

Inflation rate (consumer prices):

5.5% (2012 est.)

country comparison to the world: 152

6.6% (2011 est.)

Central bank discount rate:

7.25% (31 December 2012 est.)

country comparison to the world: 20

11% (31 December 2011 est.)

Commercial bank prime lending rate:

39.4% (31 December 2012 est.)

country comparison to the world: 2

43.88% (31 December 2011 est.)

Stock of narrow money:

$158.3 billion (31 December 2012 est.)

country comparison to the world: 23

$152.1 billion (31 December 2011 est.)

Stock of broad money:

$1.878 trillion (30 November 2011 est.)

country comparison to the world: 11

$1.826 trillion (31 December 2010 est.)

Stock of domestic credit:

$2.537 trillion (31 December 2012 est.)

country comparison to the world: 11

$2.247 trillion (31 December 2011 est.)

Market value of publicly traded shares:

$1.229 trillion (31 December 2011)

country comparison to the world: 10

$1.546 trillion (31 December 2010)

$1.167 trillion (31 December 2009)

Agriculture - products:

coffee, soybeans, wheat, rice, corn, sugarcane, cocoa, citrus; beef

Industries:

textiles, shoes, chemicals, cement, lumber, iron ore, tin, steel, aircraft, motor vehicles and parts, other machinery and equipment

Industrial production growth rate:

-0.3% (2012 est.)

country comparison to the world: 149

Current account balance:

-$65.13 billion (2012 est.)

country comparison to the world: 191

-$52.48 billion (2011 est.)

Exports:

$256 billion (2012 est.)

country comparison to the world: 24

$256 billion (2011 est.)

Exports - commodities:

transport equipment, iron ore, soybeans, footwear, coffee, autos

Exports - partners:

China 17.3%, US 10.1%, Argentina 8.9%, Netherlands 5.3% (2011)

Imports:

$238.8 billion (2012 est.)

country comparison to the world: 22

$226.2 billion (2011 est.)

Imports - commodities:

machinery, electrical and transport equipment, chemical products, oil, automotive parts, electronics

Imports - partners:

US 15.1%, China 14.5%, Argentina 7.5%, Germany 6.7%, South Korea 4.5% (2011)

Reserves of foreign exchange and gold:

$371.1 billion (31 December 2012 est.)

country comparison to the world: 6

$352 billion (31 December 2011)

Debt - external:

$405.3 billion (31 December 2012 est.)

country comparison to the world: 27

$382.5 billion (31 December 2011 est.)

Stock of direct foreign investment - at home:

$595.9 billion (31 December 2012 est.)

country comparison to the world: 14

$539.2 billion (31 December 2011 est.)

Stock of direct foreign investment - abroad:

$176.7 billion (31 December 2012 est.)

country comparison to the world: 24

$171.7 billion (31 December 2011 est.)

Exchange rates:

reals (BRL) per US dollar -

2.1 (2012 est.)

1.675 (2011 est.)

1.7592 (2010 est.)

2 (2009)

1.8644 (2008)

Fiscal year:

calendar year

Chapter 6: Energy

Electricity - production:

489.5 billion kWh (2010 est.)

country comparison to the world: 11

Electricity - consumption:

438.3 billion kWh (2010 est.)

country comparison to the world: 12

Electricity - exports:

1.257 billion kWh (2010 est.)

country comparison to the world: 56

Electricity - imports:

36.63 billion kWh (2010 est.)

country comparison to the world: 7

Electricity - installed generating capacity:

106.2 million kW (2010 est.)

country comparison to the world: 11

Electricity - from fossil fuels:

17.1% of total installed capacity (2010 est.)

country comparison to the world: 193

Electricity - from nuclear fuels:

1.9% of total installed capacity (2010 est.)

country comparison to the world: 31

Electricity - from hydroelectric plants:

74.7% of total installed capacity (2010 est.)

country comparison to the world: 20

Electricity - from other renewable sources:

6.3% of total installed capacity (2010 est.)

country comparison to the world: 31

Crude oil - production:

2.633 million bbl/day (2011 est.)

country comparison to the world: 12

Crude oil - exports:

533,200 bbl/day (2009 est.)

country comparison to the world: 21

Crude oil - imports:

412,500 bbl/day (2009 est.)

country comparison to the world: 20

Crude oil - proved reserves:

26 billion bbl (1 January 2013 est.)

country comparison to the world: 13

Refined petroleum products - production:

2.008 million bbl/day (2008 est.)

country comparison to the world: 10

Refined petroleum products - consumption:

2.594 million bbl/day (2011 est.)

country comparison to the world: 9

Refined petroleum products - exports:

164,300 bbl/day (2008 est.)

country comparison to the world: 35

Refined petroleum products - imports:

325,400 bbl/day (2008 est.)

country comparison to the world: 21

Natural gas - production:

24.07 billion cu m (2011 est.)

country comparison to the world: 31

Natural gas - consumption:

26.7 billion cu m (2011 est.)

country comparison to the world: 32

Natural gas - exports:

0 cu m (2011 est.)

country comparison to the world: 166

Natural gas - imports:

12.6 billion cu m (2011 est.)

country comparison to the world: 23

Natural gas - proved reserves:

416.9 billion cu m (1 January 2012 est.)

country comparison to the world: 34

Carbon dioxide emissions from consumption of energy:

453.9 million Mt (2010 est.)

country comparison to the world: 14

Chapter 7: Communications

Telephones - main lines in use:

43.026 million (2011)

country comparison to the world: 6

Telephones - mobile cellular:

244.358 million (2011)

country comparison to the world: 5

Telephone system:

general assessment: good working system including an extensive microwave radio relay system and a domestic satellite system with 64 earth stations

domestic: fixed-line connections have remained relatively stable in recent years and stand at about 20 per 100 persons; less expensive mobile-cellular technology has been a major driver in expanding telephone service to the lower-income segments of the population with mobile-cellular teledensity roughly 120 per 100 persons

international: country code - 55; landing point for a number of submarine cables, including Americas-1, Americas-2, Atlantis-2, GlobeNet, South America-1, South American Crossing/Latin American Nautilus, and UNISUR that provide direct connectivity to South and Central America, the Caribbean, the US, Africa, and Europe; satellite earth stations - 3 Intelsat (Atlantic Ocean), 1 Inmarsat (Atlantic Ocean region east),

connected by microwave relay system to Mercosur
Brazilsat B3 satellite earth station (2011)

Broadcast media:

state-run Radiobras operates a radio and a TV network;
more than 1,000 radio stations and more than 100 TV
channels operating - mostly privately owned; private
media ownership highly concentrated (2007)

Internet country code:

.br

Internet hosts:

26.577 million (2012)

country comparison to the world: 3

Internet users:

75.982 million (2009)

country comparison to the world: 4

Chapter 8: Transportation

Airports:

    4,105 (2012)

    country comparison to the world: 2

Airports - with paved runways:

    total: 713

    over 3,047 m: 7

    2,438 to 3,047 m: 28

    1,524 to 2,437 m: 174

    914 to 1,523 m: 449

    under 914 m: 55 (2012)

Airports - with unpaved runways:

    total: 3,392

    1,524 to 2,437 m: 91

    914 to 1,523 m: 1,648

    under 914 m: 1,653 (2012)

Heliports:

    13 (2012)

Pipelines:

    condensate/gas 62 km; gas 13,514 km; liquid petroleum gas 352 km; oil 3,729 km; refined products 4,684 km (2010)

Railways:

    total: 28,538 km

    country comparison to the world: 10

broad gauge: 5,627 km 1.600-m gauge (467 km electrified)

standard gauge: 194 km 1.440-m gauge

narrow gauge: 22,717 km 1.000-m gauge (2008)

Roadways:

total: 1,580,964 km

country comparison to the world: 4

paved: 212,798 km

unpaved: 1,368,166 km

note: does not include urban roads (2010)

Waterways:

50,000 km (most in areas remote from industry and population) (2012)

country comparison to the world: 3

Merchant marine:

total: 109

country comparison to the world: 50

by type: bulk carrier 18, cargo 16, chemical tanker 7, container 13, liquefied gas 11, petroleum tanker 39, roll on/roll off 5

foreign-owned: 27 (Chile 1, Denmark 3, Germany 6, Greece 1, Norway 3, Spain 12, Turkey 1)

registered in other countries: 36 (Argentina 1, Bahamas 1, Ghana 1, Liberia 20, Marshall Islands 1, Panama 3, Singapore 9) (2010)

Ports and terminals:

cargo ports (tonnage): Ilha Grande (Gebig), Paranagua, Rio Grande, Santos, Sao Sebastiao, Tubarao

container ports (TEUs): Santos (2,677,839), Itajai (693,580)

oil terminals: DTSE/Gegua oil terminal, Guaiba Island terminal, Guamare oil terminal

Transportation - note:

the International Maritime Bureau reports that the territorial and offshore waters in the Atlantic Ocean remain a significant risk for piracy and armed robbery against ships; 2010 saw an 80% increase in attacks over 2009; numerous commercial vessels were attacked and hijacked both at anchor and while underway; crews were robbed and stores or cargoes stolen

Chapter 9: Military

Military branches:

Brazilian Army (Exercito Brasileiro, EB), Brazilian Navy
(Marinha do Brasil (MB), includes Naval Air and Marine
Corps (Corpo de Fuzileiros Navais)), Brazilian Air Force
(Forca Aerea Brasileira, FAB) (2011)

Military service age and obligation:

21-45 years of age for compulsory military service;
conscript service obligation - 9 to 12 months; 17-45 years
of age for voluntary service; an increasing percentage of
the ranks are "long-service" volunteer professionals;
women were allowed to serve in the armed forces
beginning in early 1980s when the Brazilian Army became
the first army in South America to accept women into
career ranks; women serve in Navy and Air Force only in
Women's Reserve Corps (2001)

Manpower available for military service:

males age 16-49: 53,350,703

females age 16-49: 53,433,918 (2010 est.)

Manpower fit for military service:

males age 16-49: 38,993,989

females age 16-49: 44,841,661 (2010 est.)

Manpower reaching militarily significant age annually:

male: 1,733,168

female: 1,672,477 (2010 est.)

Military expenditures:

1.7% of GDP (2009)

<u>country comparison to the world</u>: 85

Chapter 10: Transnational Issues

Disputes - international:

uncontested boundary dispute between Brazil and Uruguay over Braziliera/Brasiliera Island in the Quarai/Cuareim River leaves the tripoint with Argentina in question; smuggling of firearms and narcotics continues to be an issue along the Uruguay-Brazil border; Colombian-organized illegal narcotics and paramilitary activities penetrate Brazil's border region with Venezuela

Illicit drugs:

second-largest consumer of cocaine in the world; illicit producer of cannabis; trace amounts of coca cultivation in the Amazon region, used for domestic consumption; government has a large-scale eradication program to control cannabis; important transshipment country for Bolivian, Colombian, and Peruvian cocaine headed for Europe; also used by traffickers as a way station for narcotics air transshipments between Peru and Colombia; upsurge in drug-related violence and weapons smuggling; important market for Colombian, Bolivian, and Peruvian cocaine; illicit narcotics proceeds are often laundered through the financial system; significant illicit financial activity in the Tri-Border Area (2008)

Other Key Facts™ Titles

Key Facts on Iraq

Key Facts on Indonesia

Key Facts on South Korea

All Key Facts™ Titles are

Available at www.Amazon.com

THE INTERNATIONALIST®

2013

www.internationalist.com

www.ingramcontent.com/pod-product-compliance
Lightning Source LLC
Chambersburg PA
CBHW051256170526
45165CB00004B/1740